Unexplained Conspiracy Theories

Hello my name is Eric Bowden and over the last few years I have written several books on the subject of video games in addition to also writing a book on Conspiracies.

The book has sold quite well and literally 1 person has asked me to write another and who am I to disappoint my readers (comedy).

With that in mind I have written about some other Conspiracies that due to time constraints were not in the original book such as the murder of popular TV presenter Jill Dando, the missing Flight MH370 and of course the whole Covid 19 thing.

Right now we are living in an age where the truth is getting more and more subjective and there is literally no news source that you can trust and as a result more and more people are beginning to question the official narrative and that is in my opinion a good thing.

In this hardback edition I have also included the entirety of the original book so if anybody did not get chance to read that then they can do so here (lucky people).

I hope you enjoy this book as much as I enjoyed writing it and if you will excuse me I am just about to get on board my black helicopter (joking).

Oklahoma City Bombing

On April 19 1995 Timothy McVeigh (who was a former soldier and served in the Iraq War) carried out a vile terrorist attack on the Alfred P Murrah Federal Building in Oklahoma City.

The resulting attacked killed 168 people and injured a further 680 more, the Federal Building was severely damaged and had to be totally demolished as a result.

Timothy McVeigh carried out the attack by renting a Ryder Truck and filling it with huge amounts of fertilizer and racing car fuel. On the morning of the attack Timothy McVeigh parked the truck near the drop off zone for the Day Care Centre of the Federal Building, he then lit a 5 minute fuse before making good his escape.

However he was very soon arrested for driving a car without a license plate (so hardly a mastermind). The highway patrolman noticed that Timothy McVeigh had a concealed firearm and promptly took him into custody, little did the patrolman know at this stage that the man he had just arrested was responsible for the biggest ever domestic Terrorist attack on the US mainland.

Soon after this dreadful attack McVeigh was charged with 160 State offenses and a further 11 Federal offenses, he was found guilty in 1997 and was finally executed by a lethal injection in April of 2001.

The question still remains however, could a very limited individual such as Timothy McVeigh really carry out such an attack on his own? Surely not in fact the FBI were for a time looking for at least one more co conspirator before eventually dropping this line of inquiry and focused on building a case against McVeigh alone.

A great many witnesses at the time of the bombing claimed to have seen Timothy McVeigh with at least one other man on the very morning of the attack.

Interestingly McVeigh was given a polygraph test by his legal defense team, he managed to pass on every question except for whether anybody else was involved in the attacks.

Some time later 2 known friends of McVeigh were arrested on suspicion of helping and sheltering him. Michael Fortier was sentenced to 12 years but Terry Nichols was sentenced to life imprisonment (although neither man matched the description of the second man seen by multiple witnesses on the day of the attacks).

So if there were other people involved in the planning of the Oklahoma Bombing who were they? And what on earth was their motivation for such a callous attack?

Well for me at least the most likely suspects are members of the Militant Far Right, indeed there was one such group who have since fallen under suspicion namely that of the Aryan Republic Army (bunch of freaks).

This group were led by Richard Guthrie and Peter Langan and were known bank robbers and white Supremacists, the whereabouts of McVeigh often coincided with were the gang were known to be. Furthermore McVeigh had told friends about a gang he was involved with in the mid west, many people believe that he was radiated by members of this group who encouraged the simple minded McVeigh to carry out such an attack.

If this was the case then why the cover up? Well for one thing it would be hugely embarrassing for the FBI that they could not stop this plot in its tracks despite apparently having several men on the inside of such groups.

The FBI did actually launched an internal investigation into attacks way back in 2004, the results of this inquiry have yet to be made public (big surprise there).

Area 51

Area 51 is the name generally given to a United States Air Force base in the state of Nevada.

The Government usually refers to Area 51 as Groom Lake or even Homey Airport and officially it is listed as a Training Range.

However a great many people think that there is much more to it than that!

The entire area is a no-fly zone which makes it very difficult to see what is really going on (I suppose that is the point really). The Military presence in this area would suggest that there is far more going on here than being merely a Training Range.

People in the area say that the security measures are overly excessive including huge fences, hundreds of armed guards and thousands of security cameras. Furthermore there are warning signs in the surrounding areas threatening deadly force to any potential intruders.

So what on earth is so important at Area 51 that such Soviet style security measures are needed?

Many people think that the Military test new and experimental weaponry and aircrafts at the base. However many others believe that there is an Extra Terrestrial element involved.

The theory goes that the US Government use Area 51 as a research facility for the investigation of UFOs possibly attempting to reverse engineer some crashed Alien spacecrafts (such as the alleged craft that crash landed in Roswell way back in 1947).

Another chilling theory suggests that captured Extra Terrestrials are taken to Area 51 to be interrogated and possibly even tortured (like an Alien version of Guantanamo Bay).

Hopefully in time the American public will be told the truth about the rather unusual activity that has been taking place here for many decades (although probably not).

HAARP

HAARP or High Frequency Active Auroral Research Program is a project that was designed to study the potential effects and uses of the upper most section of the atmosphere (referred to as the Ionosphere).

HAARP is located in a very remote section of the Alaskan wilderness and as a result not many people can get to within 20 miles of it. However those that do manage to get close enough to see it with their own eyes are greeted with a rather terrifying sight of huge rows of gargantuan antennas pointing out towards space.

Many people believe that there is much more going on here than merely studying the Ionosphere and who could blame them.

There are several theories about the true purpose of such a facility but the most popular one involves potential weather control. This theory suggests that the US Government uses HAARP as a weapon to manipulate world events to its own advantage (such as the horrific Tsunami that struck on Boxing Day 2004 in Indonesia).

Many witnesses in this area claimed to have seen thousands of US Marines arrive in Aceh (an oil rich area of Indonesia) immediately after the tragic event. Many people have speculated that this was carried out in order for the US Government to negotiate a very favorable and potentially lucrative oil deal with the rather chaotic Indonesian Government.

Other strange weather events are often believe to have been influenced by HAARP include the horrendous Hurricane Katrina which destroyed large area of New Orleans in 2005 and even the terrible earthquake that occurred in China in 2008.

Other people believe that HAARP is also used as a mind control device to help dumb down the public enough so they actually believe what their own government tells them (this explains why they voted for George W Bush as President).

Yitzhak Rabin

Born in 1922 Yitzhak Rabin was a former soldier who eventually made his way into politics and eventually the office of Prime Minister of Israel.

Yitzhak Rabin was extremely popular and was able to achieve a peaceful end of hostilities with the Palestinians in a deal know as 'The Oslo Accords'.

Sadly however this peace was not to last as Mr Rabin was assassinated after a peace rally in Tel Aviv in late 1995.

The official story was that a young Israeli student by the name of Yigal Amir was very angry about Mr Rabin giving some concessions to the Palestinians and as a direct result shot him dead.

To a great many people however this explanation is a little too neat and it is very likely that there is much about this assassination we do not yet know.

Not long after Mr Rabin was killed an Israeli newspaper called Hatzofeh published a story regarding a man by the name of Uzi Barkan.

Uzi Barkan was a well known conspiracy theorist who believed that the Israeli Secret Service had ordered the murder of Mr Rabin. Soon after the Israeli Government published a special report into the assassination which strongly suggested that whilst Yoga Amir pulled the trigger he may have been encouraged too by Shin Bet (a former Secret Service Operative).

Another person of interest here is a well known right wing extremist called Avishai Raviv. Indeed Avishai Raviv was around this time taking rather impressionable youngsters on weekend holidays and then brainwashing them with some of his radical beliefs, one of those youngsters was Yigal Amir.

This would appear to all but confirm that there was a rather considerable conspiracy to murder Mr Rabin and pull out of 'The Oslo Accords' and in the process tear up the peace treaty with the Palestinians which has indirectly led us to the current bloodbath in this region going on right now (at the time of writing this book in early 2024).

Even now there are large parts of the special report into Mr Rabin death that are unavailable to both the general public and even to the Israeli Government, all the while that this remains the case it is highly likely that we will never know the full facts behind this awful murder.

Flight MH370

On March 8 2014 Malaysia Airlines Flight MH370 mysteriously vanished with the all of the 227 passengers and 12 crew members sadly all presumed dead.

Despite a huge search and rescue effort being made in the immediate aftermath the airliner could not be located, indeed an area in excess of 46,000 square miles of ocean was searched but not a trace of the stricken airliner could be found.

Well over a year later a number of pieces of the missing MH370 were found washed ashore in the area around the Western Indian Ocean.

To this day however nobody can really even to begin to explain what on earth had happened here, that being said there are a number of possible theories that have been put forward in an effort to finally solve this mystery and bring a sense of closure to the relatives and friends of those presumed dead.

One of the most popular theories currently doing the runs involves Flight MH370 being shot down accidentally in a Military Exercise possibly in the area of the South China Sea.

Another possible explanation could be some sort of plane hijacking, of course the problem here is that surely the hijackers would have been in contact with the authorities at some stage to negotiate their terms.
Some people put forward a theory involving the CIA (Central Intelligent Agency), this theory goes along the lines of Flight MH370 for some reason being diverted to land on a small British overseas island in the Indian Ocean (Diego Garcia). This theory continues that the CIA must have wanted something or even someone onboard.

Yet another possible explanation could be that a crew member carried out a deliberate and malicious attack whilst aboard the airliner. The Authorities did check on the social media accounts of all the crew but there was nothing suspicious to indicate that this theory had any credence.

Sadly now 10 years on we are no closer to finding out what really happened to Flight MH370, hopefully one day some evidence is bought forward to finally solve the puzzle and bring answers to the love ones of the fallen crew members and passengers.

Martin Luther King

On the 4th of April 1968 legendary civil rights campaigner The Reverend Dr Martin Luther King was shot dead whilst attending a conference in Memphis regarding the rights of sanitation workers.

As is nearly always the case with assassinations it was apparently all the work of a lone wolf (in this case a small time crook by the name of James Earl Ray).

James Earl Ray had a long history of criminality but usually it involved minor thefts and not gun crime. Ray actually pleaded guilty before his trial started in an effort to avoid being executed.

Ray would later claim he had been set up by a gun smuggler but that could never been proved one way or another.

The odd thing is that James Earl Ray was actually arrested not in the USA but in London, he was caught at Heathrow Airport with false documentation. Interestingly he was on his way to Rhodesia (modern day Zimbabwe) to start training as a mercenary.

Ray was in addition to being a petty thief a white supremacist which could account for his hatred for Dr King but how did such a limited individual like Ray manage to get to London without being detected? After all there was a nation wide manhunt across the entire United States and yet he somehow manages to skillfully avoid them!

James Earl Ray was according to one of his friends in contact with a money man based in Canada known as 'The Fat Man'. This person gave Ray thousands of dollars and helped him obtain false papers to escape to Europe.

This would suggest that Ray was simply carrying out the murder of Dr King for money, but if this is true who put him up to it? And for what reason?

Well there are several prime suspects here including the CIA, in 1977 The House Select Committee on Assassinations looked into the claim that James Earl Ray had been supplied with fake identity papers by a CIA agent and heavily encouraged to carry out the shooting. No evidence was found but many people think that is highly likely to have happened.

Another person suspected to have been involved is local Memphis cafe owner loyd Jowers.

Jowers later claimed to have hosted a meeting where local government officials, local police and members of the mafia arranged the murder of Dr King.

Probably the best suspect in my opinion would be FBI director J Edgar Hoover. Hoover hated Dr King with a passion and wrongly felt that he was a security risk to the country.

The well respected Reverend Jesse Jackson (a close friend of Dr King) was actually standing next to Dr King when the murder happened, he is in no doubt that the FBI were heavily involved in the assassination.

He believed with some justification that James Earl Ray lacked the intelligence and the resources needed to carry out such a professional hit.

The FBI have agreed to publish all their documents relating to the organizations surveillance of Dr King and other files relating to their investigation into the murder.

Hopefully this will shed some light on the untimely death of one of the greatest men of the last century.

Flat Earth

Is the Earth really flat? Well no probably not but that does not stop many people from thinking otherwise.

The theory goes that NASA and other government bodies are covering up the truth about our planet. These people go by the name of "Flat Earthers" and believe that the world is flat because when you walk down the street it feels flat, it really is as simple as that for many people.

This movement really began when a well known 19th century English writer by the name of Samuel Rowsbotham published a very small book entitled Zetetic Astronomy.

In this book Rowsbotham concluded that the Earth is likely to be disc shaped with the North Pole actually in the very centre of the world with walls of ice around its perimeter, he also strongly believed that the sun, moon and all the other planets in our solar system were in fact only a few hundreds miles above the Earth.

Although this might sound rather crazy this movement has really gained popularity in more recent times with the International Flat Earth Research Society of America being revived in 2004 and boasting thousands of members.

So popular has this theory become that well known Astrophysicist Neil deGrasse Tyson was forced into debunking the Flat Earth story many times on Social Media.

I think the question here is why would NASA be attempting to cover up the Flat Earth theory if it were true?

Another question would relate to gravity, if the Earth was really flat how would we explain what is happening when an object falls to the ground?

Until the "Flat Earthers" can provide satisfactory answers for these questions I think this theory has very little credence.

Jeffrey Epstein

On 10th August 2019 vile sex offender Jeffrey Epstein was found dead in his prison cell, where he was awaiting his upcoming trial.

Epstein was no ordinary sex fiend however rather he was formally a billionaire with ties to many important and famous people (such as Prince Andrew and Bill Clinton among many others).

Epstein was originally arrested back in 2008 and duly convicted of soliciting a prostitute and for procuring an underage age for prostitution. Possibly due to his network of friends in high places he served only 13 months in prison.

Fast forward to 2019 Epstein was arrested once more this time on charges of sex trafficking dozens of underage girls in both New York and Florida.

Nobody would mourn the loss of such a disgusting sex offender but did Epstein really take his own life? Or was he murdered in order to protect the identity of other high profile perverts?

Members of Epstein legal defect team were very suspicious of his suicide and launched their own investigation. Their investigation came to the conclusion that Epstein was strangled by person or persons unknown.

Not long before his death Epstein had boasted to a friend that he had some very incriminating information about several people who were all in the public eye, he was going to reveal all of this at his trial (sadly he did not get the chance).

We will likely never known the full facts of what really happened to Epstein or perhaps more importantly we will never known the incriminating evidence he had on several other high profile sex fiends.

9/11 Terror Attacks

At the time of the September 11 2001 Terror Attacks I was working at a small toy shop in Dover, Kent. I was off every

Tuesday which just so happened to fall on 11 September.

I was flicking through the TV channels at around 1.45pm and I stumbled upon a newsflash about a plane (American Airlines Flight 11) crashing into one of the World Trade Centre buildings in New York.

At first the news came across as if it were some sort of terrible accident but very soon it became clear that it really was no accident.

Barely a few minutes later a second plane (United Airlines Flight 175) smashed into the second World Trade Centre building, I will never forget seeing this as it was the moment that life changed for us all and not for the better.

In a matter of months various war hawks in the Bush Administration and in Tony Blair's Labour Government were already talking about invading Iraq again (despite there being zero evidence of their involvement), not to mention draconic new 'Anti Terrorism' laws designed to cut down on civil liberties and protest. I remember that quite often if anybody spoke out about these new laws they were immediately branded as being a 'Traitor' (this was straight out of the Nazi playbook with regards to the Reichstag fire).

Not long after the second plane had hit we were then informed that a third plane (American Airlines 77) had struck The Pentagon (Headquarters of The United States Department of Defense).

Next we were told that a fourth plane had gone missing and had apparently crash landed in a field near Shankesville in Somerset County in Pennsylvania. It was though that the passengers of the fourth plane (United Airlines Flight 93) had managed to overpower the hijackers and had as a result forced the plane to crash land short of its intended target (which was believed to have been The White House).

Around this time tragically the first World Trade Centre Tower (North Tower) that was struck by a plane began to collapse resulting in the horrific death of a great many innocent people.

Soon after The South Tower building also collapsed and rather more bizarrely World Trade Centre Building Number 7 also collapsed despite not being hit with a plane. Officially this building collapse was put down to 'Fire' making it the only building in recorded history to totally collapse in this way!

The final death toll at the end of this most awful day was well in excess of 3000 people, a very very sad day not just for The United States but for the entire world.

Within a few hours of these horrific events several news network both in America and Britain began to put the blame squarely at the feet of Osama Bin Laden and his Al-Qaeda Terror Network.

The irony is that Al-Qaeda and the ghastly Bin Laden were trained and funded by The United States (via The CIA) as a sort of freedom fighting unit in Afghanistan in order to fight against the invading Soviet Union army in the late 1970s and early 1980s.

The double irony was when president George W Bush stated that The USA would target anybody who funded and aided 'Terrorist Organizations' maybe he should have started with his own political party and indeed his own father former President George H W Bush!

Also by some amazing coincidence on the morning of September 11 2001 The National Reconnaissance Office (they are largely responsible for America's

Reconnaissance Satellites) were wargaming carrying out a training exercise simulating commercial airlines smashing into buildings!

That was the reason given for the almost complete lack of US Airforce planes in the New York and Washington DC area on the day of the attacks.

Switching focus for a moment on to the Pentagon (sadly 125 people lost their lives here), officially the story is that an airplane (American Airlines Flight 77) crashed into The Pentagon sling through 3 poles in the car park before crashing into the first floor of The Pentagon exploding Into a fireball as a direct result.

However according to experts in this field (including a great number of engineers and architects) the damage that was done to The Pentagon was far more consistent with a missile strike as opposed to a commercial airliner. A large number of witnesses in the immediate area also described seeing a missile and not an airliner.

Interestingly the day before the attacks Donald Rumsfeld (who was the then US Secretary of Defense) stated that he could not account for 2.3 Trillion dollars missing from The Pentagon budget, of course the day after these records were rather conveniently destroyed ending the potential investigation.

Barely a month after the attacks The US Patriot Act was signed into law by President George W Bush. This Act massively cut down the rights and civil liberties of US citizens.

The Patriot Act also allowed the US Government to massively increase the level of surveillance on its own people with phone tapping especially being hugely increased. It also bought in a very insidious new law allowing the indefinite imprisonment of citizens often without reason or without a trial.

The Patriot Act was over 300 pages long and in my opinion and the opinion of a great many others the law was likely written some time before and the US Government were simply waiting for the right 'Disaster' to happen to help justify the bringing in this rather oppressive new policy.

Now the official story says the attacks were carried out by 19 plane hijackers, 15 of the hijackers were from Saudi Arabia, 2 were from United Arab Emirates, 1 from Egypt and 1 from Lebanon and so it makes perfect sense for the USA and UK to invade Iraq!

I really hope that one day the public get to know the full facts of what really happened on September 11 2001 as the official story makes very little sense.

God bless all those who died on that most fateful day and the hundreds of thousands more who have died during the various illegal wars in the immediate aftermath.

Who was the Zodiac Killer?

In the late 1960s and early 1970s residents of California were terrorized by a cowardly gunman who killed at least 5 people and attempted to kill at least 2 more.

He was known as 'The Zodiac Killer' (or just plain 'The Zodiac') because he used to write to both the police and the press boasting about committing the murders whilst leaving vague clues about his identity usually in the form of Cryptograms (a sort of puzzle containing short encrypted texts).

In his letters 'The Zodiac; comes across as a real sad and actually he claimed to have killed 37 people.

He shot and killed a teenage courting couple in late 1968, followed that up with shooting another round couple in July 1969 (although happily on this occasion one of the victims actually survived), then he brutally stabbed a yet another young couple in September 1969 (once more one of the victims did pull through) and then finally in December 1969 he shot dead a cab driver.
However, during the final murder 'The Zodiac' was seen clearly by 3 teenagers who actually phoned the police whilst the murder was being committed.

The teenagers were able to give police a very clear description of the killer - white man 35 to 45 years old - 5ft 10 inches tall - stocky build.

At last the police had at least something to go on, but sadly despite a huge manhunt (indeed San Francisco Police Department actually had over 2500 possible suspects) 'The Zodiac' was never bought to justice.

The sad did however continue to write to both police and the press alike, he would often threaten to carry out further murders but thankfully he never carried them out.

Over the years there have been a great many suspects including oddball Arthur Leigh Allen who fitted the description that the teenage witnesses had given police perfectly. Sadly the police were never really able to build much of a case against him although the fiend was sentenced to jail time a few years later for sexually assaulting a child.

Another strong suspect at the time was a filmmaker by the name of Richard Gaikowski who also fitted the description very well and like Arthur Leigh Allen was a rather odd individual (he was lated committed to a Mental Asylum for 3 years in which time there were no further 'Zodiac' letters written). However his friends insisted that at the time of the murders he was living in New York and so no further action could be taken.

More recently a new suspect emerged called Gary Francis Post, he was arrested for domestic violence towards his wife and eventually committed to a Mental Hospital in Napa. Whilst he was clearly an awful human being there does not appear to be any real evidence linking him to the murders at present.

So who was 'The Zodiac'? Sadly we may never know although the California Department of Justice still has an active case file on all of these murders and with the recent advances in technology maybe one day we can unmask this coward!

Men in Black

Not to be confused with the Tommy Lee Jones and Will Smith movies Men in Black are a terming Phenomenon who allegedly intimidate anybody who reports contact with either Aliens or UFOs.

Often thee Men in Black (or MIB) pay a visit to somebody who has recently had an unexplained experience and try to scare them into silence.

Sometimes these MIB will arrive in a pristine but often very old black car or even worse may arrive in an unmarked black helicopter.

People who have been unfortunate enough to encounter these MIB often describe them as a little odd looking, being exceptionally tall and rather more chillingly seem to talk without even moving their lips.

One witness believed that the MIB he encountered were able to read his mind!

If the witnesses refuse to be intimidated the MIB abruptly leave and instead pester the poor witness with relentless phone calls at all hours of the day and night until eventually the witness agrees to drop their account.

So just who are these MIB? Are they possibly agents of the Government trying to suppress information about possible Alien visitations and possible abduction? Or even more sinister are they actual Aliens maybe dressed as humans attempting to cover their own tracks.

In more recent years the amount of MIB encounters seemed to have fallen quite sharply, perhaps this is due to the popularity of the hit movie franchise or maybe because almost everybody has a camera on their phone these days they are more reluctant to break cover!

The Whitechapel Murders

I don't know for sure who Jack the Ripper was but I know he was not married, after all I never saw him with the same woman twice! (Sorry bad taste).

Jack the Ripper was the moniker given to the fiend who murdered at least 5 woman between August and November of 1888.

The name Jack the Ripper came from a letter that was allegedly written by the killer to a local newspaper although in all likelihood it was written by a journalist attempting to sell more papers.

The first murder was carried out on Friday 31 August 1888, a local prostitute Mary Ann Nichols was found in the early hours with her throat savagely cut with her abdomen cut wide open.

Sadly the murder of prostitutes at the time was nothing unusual, but what was unusual was the sheer depravity and ferocity of the attack.

Just one week later another prostitute was murdered in near identical fashion, the unfortunate woman was Annie Chapman. If anything this attack was even more grotesque with several organs being removed including the Uterus and sections of her bladder.

The beast would soon strike again, in fact he would murder two woman in the same night on Sunday 30 September 1888 both Catherine Eddowes and Elizabeth Stride.

Elizabeth Stride was murdered first but whilst her throat was cut identically to the previous murders there were no other mutilations to speak of, this would suggest the killer was disturbed during the attack and had fled the scene.

Sadly his work was not yet finished as the body of poor Catherine Eddowes was soon discovered.

Catherine Eddies had her throat cut in identical fashion to the earlier victims in addition to several disgusting mutilations to her body including an almost total disfigurement of her face and the removal of her kidneys and uterus.

According to a Police Surgeon these mutilations would have taken at least 5 minutes or more to carry out suggesting that the killer was clearly confident that he would not be interrupted.

Interestingly very close to where the body of Catherine Eddowes was found there was a message written on a wall that stated "The Juwes are the men that will not be blamed for nothing!".

Whether or not they were written by the killer or not is unclear but the then Police Commissioner Sir Charles Warren ordered it to be removed as he feared an Anti Semitism backlash.

Sadly the killer was not yet finished as on Friday 9 November 1888 he struck again but this time he murdered the lady inside her own dwelling.
Mary Ann Kelly was the victim here and she was butchered so badly as to be almost totally unrecognizable.

Here the beast had actually cut our Mary Jane Kelly's heart, in addition to this he had removed one of her breasts, Both her kidneys and her uterus and placed them above her head.

It is hard to fully understand the rage that must have been flowing through this fiends body to carry out such an attack.

As suddenly as the murder had begun they stopped after the murder of Mary Jane Kelly, there were several more murders around the area in the following few years but none of them were quite the same as those carried out by Jack the Ripper.

So why did he stop? Was he arrested for another crime? Did he flee the area? Dick his sick mind finally cave in after carrying out such heinous acts?

Over the years there have been a great many theories put forward as to who Jack the Ripper was including Royal Doctor Sir William Gull, famous painter Walter Sickett, Queen Victoria's grandson Prince Albert Victor to more plausible suspects such as local man (and occasional lover of Mary Jane Kelly) Jospeh Barnett , escaped lunatic James Kelly and American oddball Dr Francis Tumblety.

In my opinion the killer was none of the above, the problem is that largely thanks to Hollywood Movies and Television Drama series we somehow have this image of Jack the Ripper as being a sort of charismatic super villain. The truth however is that whoever he was he was simply a cowardly loser who took out his frustrations on vulnerable woman who could not possibly fight back. He was almost certainly such an insignificant person that he flew under the radar, the only reason he got away was simply down to getting very lucky a few times, case in point the Yorkshire Ripper (Peter Sutcliffe).

Peter Sutcliffe should have been caught years before he eventually was but he was such a total no mark that nobody ever really suspected him. I believe the same would almost certainly be true of Jack the Ripper.

If anyone would like to know more about this subject I would highly recommend another book entitled 'The Complete History of Jack the Ripper' written by the late Phillip Sugden.

Big Cats in Britain

Over the past 40 years there have been a number of sightings in Britain of a large catlike creature that is definitely not naive to the British Isles.

These sightings have ben reported all over the country but the majority of them seem to occur down in the West Country especially the area surrounding Bodmin Moor in Cornwall.

There are a small number of very convincing photographs of these big cats (most of which appear to show a Puma or possibility a Panther like creature).

At one point during the 1990s there were so many sightings of big and wild cats that questions were asked in Parliament and as a result an Official Enquiry was opened.

Sadly the Official Enquiry which was carried out by the Ministry of Agriculture, Fisheries and Food concluded that there was no evidence of big cats roaming free in the British countryside.
One theory which could help explain least some of the big cat sightings relates to 'The Dangerous Wild Animals Act of 1976'. This Act made it illegal to own certain species of animals without obtaining a special license.

As a direct result of this Act it has been speculated that a great many owners of big cats simply released their dangerous pets into the British Countryside.

I believe that this may account for the majority of cases as almost all sightings took place after 1976.

However there are some people who believe that this is not actually the case and the big wild cats that have been encountered are actually native to Britain but were thought to be long extinct.

The truth will be revealed soon enough I think as we build more and more on our ever decreasing countryside we are surely bound to encounter these big cats in the not too distant future.

Moon Landing 1969

In July of 1969 NASA (National Aeronautics and Space Administration) successfully landed a spacecraft on the surface of the moon.

Astronauts including Neil Armstrong, Buzz Aldrin and John Glen actually walked on the surface of the Moon before a global audience of more than 500 million people.

But were things quite as they seemed?

Well just looking at the photographic evidence of the day several strange things immediately raised suspicions.

For starters there were no visible stars seen in any of the photographs taken on the Moon surface, this immediately sparked rumors that the Moon landings were actually faked and were likely filmed in a studio.

Another oddity relates to the American flag photo which appeared to show the flag being ruffled by wind (this is not possible as the Moon does not have any weather due to the lack of a significant atmosphere). As a result a great many people believed that this was likely filmed on Earth rather than the Moon.

Also there were no visible marks from where the Spacecraft landed and the shadows of the astronauts and objects were not parallel (they should have been parallel due to the Sun being the only light source).

Finally a photo showing a large chunk of Moon rock appears to show a large C near the top of it leading to some people suggesting the C was actually a studio prop.

So if the Moon landings were fake why? Well if you look back at this era the Cold War was really at its height and it was very important that America reached the Moon before the Soviet Union did for propaganda reasons.

Also the Moon landings were also a very good distraction from the increasingly unpopular Vietnam War.

I personally believe that the Moon landings were most probably faked (or at the very least the photographs certainly were) but going against that I do accept that if that were the case all the astronauts would need to be onboard with this lie and for that matter so would all the employees of NASA (at the time of the Moon landings that would be several thousand people).

Bigfoot and Yeti

For hundreds of years in North America people claim to have seen a huge and muscular human like creature covered in fur.

Sightings of this creature (often referred to as Bigfoot or Sasquatch) date back to the 16th century when Spanish explorers encountered this mysterious being.

The Native American tribes often talked of mysterious hairy creatures especially in the North West Pacific areas of the United States.

In more recent times there have been a plethora of sightings and one very famous video taken by Roger Patterson and Robert Gimlin showing a female Bigfoot walking away from the camera (captured in 1967 in a woodland area of Northern California).

This footage is extremely impressive and despite numerous attempts by various people to discredit the film it still stands today as the very best evidence available.

It is not just in the United States that these creatures have been sighted as a very similar bing has been seen around the Himalayan Mountain Range in Asia.

Locally these creatures are referred to as either a 'Yeti' or an 'Abominable Snowman' and the descriptions given of these beings is almost identical to the sightings of 'Bigfoot'.

There is a wealth of witness statements here including one from legendary explorer and adventurer Sir Edmund Hilary who witnessed very unusual large footprints in the snow in 1952. Several years later he returned to the area and collected a scalp from a supposed 'Yeti'.

Hilary then took a sample of the scalp back to London for testing which actually revealed that it was not from a bear or any other known species!

Sadly though there is no photographic proof of these beings as of now that can help prove the existence of the 'Yeti' one way or another.

There has even been a few reports of 'Bigfoot' type creatures in Britain in more recent years although sightings are still relatively rare compared with the United States.

So what could this mysterious creature be? Could it be an unknown animal species? Or is it maybe a missing link between present humans and cave men? Or is it simply practical jokers dressing up in a furry suite?

Well at this moment the jury is still out, personally though I think something is out there though I also do accept that until a body is found many people will remain skeptical.

Is The Megalodon Shark Still Active?

The Megalodon was a huge shark measuring well over 60ft in length and weighing up to 50 metric tonnes.

Previously the Megalodon was believed to belong to the same family as the Great White Shark but many scientists now believe that it was much more closely related to Mackeral Sharks.

Megalodon was thought to have become extinct around 3 million years ago, but did it?

Well it well worth remembering that at present we have only really explored around 5% of the worlds oceans (despite the oceans making up more than 70% of the entire planet) so in theory all manner of weird and wonderful creatures may be lurking in the depths.

The Megalodon was one of the fiercest and strongest predators to ever roam our oceans and if it were still out there somewhere I would advise anyone to think twice about going into the water!

So is there any real evidence to suggest that these creatures are still alive? All nothing concrete although there are a great many reports from various witness accounts largely from fisherman who reported confrontations with huge sharks that all bear a striking resemblance to Megalodon.

If these beasts were still roaming the seas it may well explain why hundreds of ships go missing each year with the sad loss of everyone on board.

Then again if such a massive species of shark were still active then surely we would have found some evidence of it (such as newer fossils or even a captured Megalodon).

Another factor which really counts against the existence of the Megalodon is the cooling of the oceans. Indeed the oceans today are much cooler than they were millions of years ago, this means that the food chain is very different today which would make the Megalodons diet very different (resulting in possible starvation).

Whilst Megalodon sharks were amazing creatures I really hope they are now extinct!

Did Adolf Hitler Escape Berlin in 1945?

Did maniac and war criminal Adolf Hitler really die in his Berlin bunker in late April of 1945? Or did he escape the carnage and eventually end up in Argentina alongside many other disgusting Nazi war criminals? Or did he flee to Britain to write for the Daily Mail (just kidding).

The official story was that on 30 April 1945 Adolf Hitler committed suicide alongside his wife Eva Braun most likely by biting down on a cyanide pill. He also apparently shot himself in the head just to be sure.

The story continues that after the alleged suicides both of their bodies were burned and later buried in shallow graves.

Soon after the bodies of these 2 disgusting human beings were dug up and later identified by the occupying Soviet Armed Forces.

However sources close to the Kremlin apparently believed that Jospeh Stalin (at the time he was President of the USSR) was convinced that Hitler had escaped and was being shielded by pro Fascist Governments either in Spain or even somewhere in South America (likely Argentina).

Stories also began to emerge during the 1950s that Adolf Hitler and Eva Braun had several body doubles and it was a pair of these body doubles that were found by the approaching Soviet forces.

There was also a plethora of sightings of the couple during the lat 1940s and throughout the 1950s mainly in the Patagonia region of Argentina.

Furthermore a former Captain in the SS Peter Erich Baumgart told a court in Germany in late 1947 that he had flew both Hitler and his new bride to Denmark from Berlin just before the city was overrun by Soviet forces.

Captain Baumgart ws paid 20,000 marks for this service, he believed that the evil couple then boarded by a flight to Spain and then eventually reached South America by submarine.

Also we know for sure that a great many Nazi was criminals did flee to South America in the aftermath of World War 2, case in point the ghastly Adolf Eichmann (who was a major organizer of the Holocaust) was captured in 1960 in Argentina by Israel Secret Service Operatives (often referred to as Mossad).

The evil Eichmann was taken back to Israel where he was put on trial and sentenced to death by hanging in 1962.

Another appalling excuse for a human being Klaus Barbie (nicknamed the Butter of Lyon) worked as a Gestapo Officer for the Nazi's in France during the German occupation was captured in Bolivia. For some strange reason he managed to escape the hangman's noose but did at least die in prison in late 1991.

With this in mind is it too much of a stretch to think that the biggest scumbag of the all would find a game somewhere in South America? I don't believe it is!

I firmly believe that he and his wife did survive the war because lets face it his sot always does! I mean how often do you hear about some War Criminal who is 112 years old and living in luxury somewhere?

Also if you look at Adolf Hitler's character it soon becomes clear that he was a huge coward! He never once went anywhere near the front where the fighting was taking place whereas the legendary Winston Churchill was always popping up near the front to chat with soldiers an help raise morale.

So if Hitler was too cowardly to visit his own men at the front would he have the courage to shoot himself in the head? Doubtful in my book!

If anyone would like to know more about this subject may I suggest a fantastic book written by Gerrard Williams and Simon Dunstan called 'Grey Wolf: The Escape of Adolf Hitler.

The Loch Ness Monster

What lurks in the icy depths of Loch Ness? Well according to a great many people a Plesiosaur (a Dinosaur thought to be long extinct).

Many people that I have spoken to on this subject always seem to think that the Loch Ness monster (known locally as just 'Nessie') is a rather recent phenomenon but in actual fact the first recorded sighting of 'Nessie' was way back in the year 565!

Loch Ness is situated in the Highland of Scotland and is a huge fresh water lake (indeed it is the second largest lake in Scotland behind only Loch Lomond) and is a very popular destination for tourists.

The area has much to offer including some of the most breathtaking views available on the entire British Isles, a very impressive 13th century castle

(Urguahart) and of course a very famous resident Dinosaur (maybe).

Over the years there have been a very high number of 'Nessie' sightings and even some very convincing photographic evidence but sadly as yet nothing which will help prove one way or the other if the creature or creatures really do exist.

If 'Nessie' is real then what is it? Could it really be a Plesiosaur? These Dinosaurs were supposed to have died out around 66 million years ago, surely if there were a small colony of these creatures in the Scottish Highlands surely we would know about it! Also Plesiosaurs were believed to be cold blooded and simply could not survive in the very cold waters of Loch Ness.

So if not a Plesiosaur what else could 'Nessie' really be? Well a former British Naval Officer named Rupert Gould put forward an interesting theory that 'Nessie' was not a Dinosaur after all but rather a long necked giant Amphibian (possibly a long necked Newt).

Others have put forward the notion that 'Nessie' could be a giant Bristleworm whilst many other people claim that there is nothing really there at all and it is merely a ploy to encourage more tourists to the area.

In my opinion however I really do think that something is there, the sheer amount of witness statements cannot be ignored.

Interestingly at the time that this book was being written (late 2023) there was huge search underway at Loch Ness involving drones, underwater sound generators and infrared cameras.

Maybe this search will settle this question once and for all.

Paul McCartney

I have been a huge fan of conspiracies for decades now and have read countless books on the subject but this particular conspiracy I only heard about relatively recently namely did Paul McCartney die in a car crash in 1966?

Admittedly there is little evidence to back up this theory (apart from his rather drab solo career over the past 40 plus years) but all the same it is fun to look into.

The rumor goes that Paul McCartney died in a car crash in 1966 and was actually replaced by a body double (quite possibly a young fan named Billy Shears). This was done to help ensure that the Beatles huge popularity continued unaffected.

There are several rather cryptic clues relating to this including on the front cover of the 'Sergeant Pepper's Lonely Hearts Club Band' album. On the front cover the number plate of the car in the foreground reads '28 IF' (McCartney would have been 28 at the time of the album release), also fellow Beatle member George Harrison was dressed as an undertaker which seemed rather out of place.

There were also some rather strange messages in various Beatle tracks when played backwards which hinted at Paul being dead (such as the verse "I buried Paul" from 'Strawberry Fields Forever").

One other clue comes from 1980 when Paul McCartney was arrested in Japan for possession of cannabis. Allegedly the fingerprints taken from Paul did not match those previously on record for him. This is at this moment unverified but it is definitely interesting nonetheless.

This conspiracy is probably not true in all honestly but it is fun to speculate.

The Reptilian Elite

Many people now believe that the majority of our elected leaders are actually reptiles in disguise. But is there any proof of this apart from Jacob Rees Mogg? (Joking)

Well apart from the bonkers decisions that they take apparently on our behalf.

According to many conspiracy writers reptile like aliens have infiltrated many of our governments disguised as humans in order to manipulate world events to their own advantage.

This particular conspiracy actually dates back thousands of years with several ancient civilizations often referring to apparent lizard men such as Sober (an Egyptian good with the head of a crocodile).

According to many conspiracy theorists the likes of Hilary Clinton , Barack Obama and George H W Bush are actually reptilian aliens in human skin.

Some theories on this subject suggest that these reptilian aliens are from a distant star system called Sigma Draconis and they have been living amongst us on Earth and even inter breeding with humans for several millennia.

These Reptiles are it is said fighting their own war against another alien race known as the Grey's.

The 'Grey's are often thought to be behind the majority of Alien Abduction cases. It has actually speculated that the Grey's are human beings from the future that have evolved but is is of courses merely guess work at this stage.

So if the reptile aliens are really here and already amongst us what is their end goal? Well nobody really seems to know for sure although it really cannot be good news can it? If their objectives were pure then surely they would come out into the open rather than hide behind such walls of secrecy.

It has to be said however that some elements of this conspiracy do sadly feature rather uncomfortable Anti Semitic tropes. Often the description of these reptilian aliens does mirror the horrible and racist descriptions of Jewish people throughout the ages (such as blood drinking and wealth and plotting).

Whilst this is an interesting subject I would advise anyone to proceed with caution on this one as it is easy to get mixed up with the wrong crowd (such as numerous far right groups on various websites).

Rudolf Hess

Rudolf Hess was a truly awful individual who was a committed Nazi and war criminal. In fact so committed a Nazi was Rudolf Hess that fellow scumbag and junkie and war criminal Adolf Hitler officially made him Deputy Fuhrer.

Rather oddly on May 10 1941 Rudolf Hess (who was also a qualified pilot) flew a small plane (a Messerchmitt BF 110) from Germany to Scotland apparently in an attempt to broker some sort of peace deal between Nazi Germany and Great Britain.

Hess had wrongly believed that the Duke of Hamilton (Douglas Hamilton) was sympathetic to the Nazi cause, which he was most certainly not!

The Duke had Rudolf Hess arrested on his arrival and Hess was then transferred to the Tower of London and then eventually onto a secure building located somewhere in in Surrey.

Hess was actually moved around Britain several more times during the war years until he eventually was sent to Nuremberg to stand trial for 'Crimes Against Humanity'.

Oddly unlike the majority of other mass murdering criminals on trial Hess did not get sentenced to death, he instead received life imprisonment. Also rather odd was how Hess did not seem to know any of the other high ranking Nazi officials that were also on trial.

At this ate rumors were rife that this person was not really Hess but rather a body double, furthermore Hess was examined in 1973 by a former Army Surgeon named Hugh Thomas.

When Hugh Thomas examined Hess he could find no trace of the bullet wounds that the real Hess was known to have picked up during the First World War in modern day Romania.

So if this person was not the real Hess who on earth was he? And what became of the real Rudolf Hess?

Well one theory was that Hess was actually shot down and killed by his own side before he had chance to even leave German airspace. Then the body double was then sent in his place to Scotland!

Not really sure what the point of this would be but then again when dealing with the Nazi's common sense usually goes out of the window.

But if this person was not the real Rudolf Hess why on earth did he happily spend the next 40 years in prison for crimes he apparently did not commit?

One final puzzle here was the nature of this person's death, Hess was found dead in his cell on August 1987. The official verdict was death by suicide (in this case hanging), however it is very unlikely that Hess could have achieved this without at least some help as he was known to suffer with terrible arthritis in his fingers which meant he could not even tie his own shoe laces.

In addition to this the handwriting found on his apparent suicide note did not match earlier writing known to have been written by Hess.

So if he really was murdered in 1987 the question is who by? And why? Also why wait over 40 years to do it? I mean by this stage he was already in his 90s so how much longer could he have lived for anyway?

Interestingly it later emerged that under the reasonably liberal leadership of Mikhail Gorbachev the Soviet Union (or USSR) was prepared to release him but Britain at the time heavily opposed his release.

So what secrets if any did this person have that could potentially embarrass Britain? And could this have been the reason why he had to be eliminated?

One other very strange thing about this case was that Rudolf Hess was adamant that he flew straight from Augsburg in Germany to just outside Kilmarnock in Scotland.

However this cannot possibly have been true as the distance between Augsburg and Kilmarnock is just over 900 miles whilst the Messerschmitt 110 that Hess used could only travel a maximum of around 565 miles before refueling. The means that Hess simply must have stopped along the way in order to refuel.

With that being said who could have helped Hess? And where exactly did the refueling take place?

One theory suggests that Admiral Canaris (Head of the German Military Intelligence Service and somewhat of an anti Nazi) helped to arrange the refueling possibly somewhere in occupied Denmark.

It has been further suggested that these 2 men were attempting some sort of coup against the Nazi High Command but I guess we will never know for sure.

Dr David Kelly

In July of 2003 Dr David Kelly (a weapons expert and scientist specializing in Biological Warfare) was found dead in the woods on Harrowdown Hill near his home in Oxfordshire.

The official story states that Dr Kelly had taken his own life by overdosing on Co-Proxamol (an Analgesic and Opiod pain killer) and for good measure slashing his own wrist with pruning knife.

But why? Well Dr David Kelly was at the time working for the Ministry of Defense as a specialist in Biological Warfare and also as a Weapons Inspector for the United Nations (UN).

A short while before his death he had a chat with the then BBC Defense and Diplomatic Correspondent Andrew Gilligan.

Dr Kelly told Andrew Gilligan that the threat of 'Weapons of Mass Destruction' were greatly exaggerated by Tony Blair and his New Labour government (with Downing Street Press Secretary Alastair Campbell especially pushing for war).

Dr David Kelly was later cross examined by some establishment no marks at a Foreign Affairs Select Committee, at this hearing Dr Kelly admitted speaking to Andrew Gilligan about the government's dodgy dossier on Iraq.

The official version of events is that soon after this Dr Kelly fell into a deep depression and this resulted in him taking his own life.

But was this what really happened? I don't think so, there are many reasons to think that Dr Kelly was likely murdered by agents of the British government.

To begin with Dr Kelly was according to friend and family members not suicidal at this time, indeed on the day of his death he was actually working from home responding to several questions from various Members of Parliament. He also spoke to his good friend Wing Commander John Clark who was able to confirm that Dr Kelly was in extremely good spirits.

Furthermore Dr Kelly actually spoke to a New York Times reporter named Judith Miller.

Judith Miller wished Dr Kelly the best of luck and he replied that he felt that "many dark actors are playing games", Dr Kelly then went on to thanks Judith Miller for supporting him.

Now does this really sound like somebody about to take their own life?

Now regarding the physical act of Dr Kelly's suicide, at the Hutton Inquiry (which was set up to look into the death of Dr David Kelly) a Forensic Pathologist said he was totally convinced that Dr Kelly had taken his own life and that nobody else was involved in his untimely death.

However many medical experts disagreed with these findings, in the Guardian newspaper 3 highly distinguished experts C. Stephen Frost, David Halpin and Searl Sennett expressed the opinion that Dr Kelly could not possibly have died in the way the official story suggests.

These experts were all of the opinion that Dr Kelly would have needed to lose a far greater amount of blood than he actually did in order to die in this manner.

Also a Forensic Toxicologist Dr Alexander Allan stated his firm belief that the amount of Co-Proxamol in Dr Kelly's system would be insufficient to result in his death.

The knife which Dr Kelly had apparently used to slash his own wrists have no fingerprints on and yet when his body was discovered he had no glove on.

Questions were also raised about the official inquiry as more than 20 important witnesses were not allowed to give their testimony including the Police Officer who led the investigation Superintendent Alan Young.
The death certificate for Dr David Kelly was not completed until 18 August 2003 over 3 weeks after his death. At that time it was the norm to complete a death certificate within 5 working days.

There were several reports from numerous sources that a helicopter was spotted landing in the immediate are where Dr David Kelly's body was discovered.

Was this helicopter linked in any way to his death? Did the helicopter actually belong to Thames Valley Police? If not who did it belong to and why were they in the immediate area where Dr Kelly's body was discovered?

None of these points were ever raised at the official inquiry and I believe it is high time that his family and friends found out what really happened to him.

It is also worth pointing out that several British politicians also questioned the official account of Dr David Kelly's death including former Liberal Democrat MP Norman Baker.

Norman Baker actually went on to write a book on the subject in 2007 entitled 'The Strange Death of David Kelly' which is well worth checking out if you wanted more depth on this issue.

Incidentally the Liberal Democrats were the only major British Political Party to completely oppose the illegal invasion of Iraq, for which they were branded 'Traitors' by the guttersnipes of the British media.

The Death of Elvis Presley

In August of 1977 the undisputed King of Rock and Roll Elvis Presley died from a drug overdose or so it is claimed.

The official story states that Elvis had accidentally overdosed on both sleeping pills and anti depressants. By this stage of his life Elvis was in very poor physical condition having lived a very indulgent lifestyle for many years.

Elvis was extremely overweight and was heavily reliant on prescription drugs to even get out of bed in the morning.

A few years before his death Elvis had overdosed on an Opiod pain reliever called Pethidine and as a result was actually in a coma for 3 days. This occurred during the time he was getting divorced and was understandingly depressed.

But around the time of his death Elvis had staged somewhat of a recovery, his music career had taken off once again and he was said to have been in extremely good spirits (he was even about to begin a major Live Tour again).

Elvis was apparently found by his fiancé Ginger Alden lying unresponsive on the bathroom floor, he was then taken to hospital soon after and pronounced dead at around 3.30pm on the afternoon of August 16 1977.

Curiously after completing an Autopsy on Elvis the Medical Examiner Jerry Francisco stated that Elvis had died of a Cardiac Arrest and definitely not of a drug overdose.

However a Forensic Pathologist named Cyril Wecht insisted that Elvis had clearly died of a drugs overdose.

The case was actually reopened in 1994 when Senior Medial Examiner Joseph Davis concluded that a heart attack was the sue of death.

Many people actually dispute that Elvis had even died at all, these people firmly believe that Elvis had faked his own death and there are a wide variety of different theories as to why he would do this.

Some people believe that Elvis had simply grown tired of fame and as a result faked his own death in order to live a quiet and normal life.

Other people think that Elvis faked his own death to avoid being killed by the Mafia (Elvis had allegedly got mixed up with some shady gangsters when attempting to organize a large property deal which went ended up going badly wrong for both Elvis and the Mafia).

Another theory involves Elvis working in secret for both the CIA and the FBI in the war of drugs, his death was staged to protect him from drug cartels hell bent on revenge.

Is there any proof of Elvis still being alive? Well right up to this very day there are hundreds of sightings of Elvis Presley in various locations around the world.

Oddly the day after Elvis had died a man looking very much like him was spotted boarding a plane to South America under the name of 'Jon Burrows'.

Interestingly 'Jon Burrows' was an alias often used by Elvis Presley for when he needed to book a hotel room without drawing any publicity.

Another strange detail is that on the day that Elvis died there were several black helicopters seen in the immediate vicinity of his Graceland mansion in Memphis, Tennessee. Many people have speculated that Elvis was picked up and flown to a remote location to start his new life.

I would love this conspiracy to be true but I fully accept that at present there is probably insufficient evidence to suggest he did not die way back in 1977.

Alien Abduction

Amazingly over 7 million people in North America believe that they have been abducted by aliens.

So what could be going on here? Could it be mental health issue? Or could it be some sort of sleep paralysis? Then gain maybe it is actually true!

Over the years there have been a great many abduction stories in the media but probably the best known I think is that of Betty and Barney Hill way back in 1961.

Betty and Barney Hill were driving on a rural highway in New Hampshire in North America on 19 September 1961. Betty saw a very bright light that she thought may have been a falling star except that it appeared to move upwards.

Soon after the bright light appeared to get much larger and much closer and so as a result Barney stopped the car in order to get a closer look. Barney at this stage believed it may be a low flying commercial aircraft in trouble but he soon changed his mind when the object very quickly changed direction and headed straight for the couple.

Betty and Barney got bak into their car and then contained to observe the object as it moved very erratically around them. Soon after the object made a beeline for them and at this point the couple got out of the car and used a pair of binoculars to get a closer look at the object.

Barney witnessed though the binoculars a number of strange looking creatures who he claimed were able to communicate with him telepathically. These beings told Barney to stay where he was!

The next memory the couple had was when they arrived back home, however they could not account for the fact that more than 7 hours had gone by.

In order to find out what exactly had happened to them Barney and Betty actually underwent a form of Hypnotic Regression. This revealed that the couple were abducted and subjected to a series of medical tests by these beings.

The couple were unharmed physically but were understandably very badly shaken up by this turn of events.

In my opinion both Betty and Barney were very reliably witnesses and certainly not the sort of people to court any publicity or controversy.

Many other people have had very similar experiences in the years since.

So what on earth is going on here?

Well one theory which I think can explain many cases of potential alien abduction is Sleep Paralysis.

Sleep Paralysis is where somebody has the felling of being awake but is unable to move or speak, this usually occurs when the person is waking up or when they are just about to fall asleep.

It is very common for people with this condition to experience very uncomfortable hallucinations (often with an entity attacking them in their bed). My own Mother suffers on occasion from this awful condition.

However Sleep Paralysis does not explain what happened to Barney and Betty Hill and so the question remains could an alien race really be abducting humans? And if they are for what purpose? Do they select targets at random or even more sinisterly do they choose their intended target in advance and simply wait for the right moment to strike?

Well one school of thought is that these aliens have made a deal with our national governments. This deal more or less says that aliens can abduct and carry out experiments on human subjects in exchange for our governments gaining access to advanced technology.

If this really is true then it certainly helps to explain the Men in Black phenomenon, this is where apparent government agents often visit people who claim to have been abducted by aliens (or maybe if they have reported seeing a UFO) and attempt to intimidate them into silence.

Looking at the sheer vastness of the universe it is certain that there are a great many intelligent life forms out there and it is surely very possible if not probable that they have visited our planet at some stage.

Having said that looking at some of our Elected Representatives I am not not if there is much intelligent on this planet!

Who Killed JFK?

President John Fitzgerald Kennedy (usually referred to as simply JFK) was the 35th President of The United States of America, he was also the youngest man ever elected as President at that time.

By and large JFK was very popular both in North America and overseas. But he did pick up a number of powerful enemies mainly due to his commitment to the Civil Rights Movement and for his reluctance to involve the USA in the Vietnamese civl war.

Well sadly on November 22 1963 in Dallas, Texas President Kennedy was assassinated whilst in his Presidential Motorcade officially by an unstable oddball by the name of Lee Harvey Oswald.

The President was shot twice, the fist bullet hit him in the back whilst the second hit in in the head.

President Kennedy was taken to Parkland Hospital where he sadly died soon after.

Lee Harvey Oswald was arrested very quickly after the FBI had found a partial handprint of his on the barrel of the murder weapon (which was a Italian Carcano M91/38 Bolt Action Rifle) which was found on the sixth floor of the nearby Texas School Book Depository building.

Oswald later shot dead a police officer who had recognized him before he was eventually cornered and then arrested at a local cinema.

Oswald would later make the claim that he did not shoot anybody and that somebody was attempting to frame him. Lee Harvey Oswald was briefly a US Marine but those who knew him at this time said he was certainly not a crack shot (which the real killer so clearly was).

After leaving the US Marines Oswald actually went to live in the Soviet Union for a time during which he became a Communist and even married a Russian woman.

Oswald was soon charged with both the murder of President Kennedy and with the murder of Police Officer Tippet.

Despite this Oswald would never see the inside of a courtroom. On November 24 1963 as Oswald was being transferred to the County Jail he was shot dead by nightclub owner Jack Ruby.

Tis sparks a number of questions namely why did Dallas police allow jack Ruby to get so close to Oswald? Especially as Jack Ruby had a gun in his hand and was shouting at the top of his voice "You killed the President, you rat!".

Jack Ruby himself died very soon afterwards apparently of Cancer so we will never know for sure what his true motivation for killing Lee Harvey Oswald really was.

The big question for me is could a man of very limited ability and intellect such as Oswald really pull something like this off? I really don't think so and if not who really carried out and organized this assassination?

Well over the years there have been a great many possible theories and suspects including the CIA. This theory goes along the lines of the CIA being incensed by President Kennedy's handling of the Bay of Pigs incident (this was essentially a failed American coup against Cuba).

The CIA had felt that the President had become a liability and as a result organized a hit against him and possibility setting up Oswald as the fall guy.

Another possible suspect would be what is known as 'The Military Industrial Complex (essentially a very powerful lobbyist group full of self serving and self interested Arms Manufacturing Corporations).

This group was desperate for a war between the United States and Vietnam, however President Kennedy was opposed to this. Almost immediately after the assassination the then Vice President Lyndon B. Johnson was sworn in as President Kennedy's replacement. One of the very fist things he did was to send troops to Vietnam which was the east polar opposite of what President Kennedy would have done.

The third viable suspect theory involves the Mafia, soon after President Kennedy came into office he started to take down organized crime groups (especially the Mafia)

Which severely affected their profits. Another reason why the Mafia hated President Kennedy was down to his reluctance to send more troops to Vietnam. The reason for this was likely due to the Mafia often importing drugs from Vietnam.

Allegedly the Mafia were concerned that the Vietnamese authorities would put a stop to their murky dealings unless a US invasion happened which would massively affect the Vietnamese government's ability to fight organized crime.

Sadly more than 60 years later we still do not know entirely what happened on that fateful day and maybe we never will. If this had occurred today the mainstream media would likely blame it on Putin! Or Prince Harry!
(Kidding)

The Strange Death of Pope John Paul 1

Born in 1912 in Italy Albino Luciano was a quiet, friendly and inoffensive man who spent the majority of his working life as a priest.

He became a priest in 1935 and eventually rose to prestigious role of Patriarch of Venice in 1969.

Despite being very well respected both inside and outside of the church it was still a great surprise to many when he was surprisingly elected as Pope in 1978.

Taking the name of John Paul 1 the new Pope began his reign by attempting to clean up the very corrupt Vatican (especially the dodgy financial dealings and possible links to organized crimes).

Turning into somewhat of a modern day reformer Pope John Paul 1 apparently wanted to relax the official church position on contraception.

This was all too much for all those self serving hypocrite that make up the majority of people associated with the Vatican and so they decided to act.

Pope John Paul 1 was found dead in his bed by his
housekeeper on August 6 1978 a mere 33 days into his reign.

The official cause of his death was given as a heart attack.

However there are several very odd things here which do not really add up. Firstly in Italian law there must be a period of at least 24 hours before a body can be embalmed after death, but in this case Pope John Paul 1 body was embalmed in less than 12 hours.

Also Italian law clearly sates that when embalming the blood and the organs of the person must be removed but here they were not.

I believe that this was done to prevent anyone from seeing if the Pope had been poisoned or not.

Another very strange detail relates to his housekeeper (a nun called Vincenza Taffarel) who found the body of Pope John Paul 1.

Vincenza Taffarel at the time said she had discovered the body of the Pope in his bathroom but later would go one to change her story saying that she had found him sat up in his bed.

Also her testimony is missing from the official Vatican report for reasons unknown.

Even today there is still no official death certificate for Pope John Paul 1. His successor would also face similar problems but thankfully had a bit more luck.

The man who stepped into Pope John Paul 1 shoes was a lovely gentleman from Poland by the name of Karol Jozef Wojtyla who became Pope John Paul 2).

Pop John Paul 2 was almost killed in 1981, a lone gunman who was mentally unstable (sounds familiar) shot at him but luckily he survived.

Many people have speculated that Pope John Paul 2 had somehow fallen foul of the powerful Masonic Lodge that controls so much of Italy (sometimes referred to as P2).

The following year another unstable lunatic (once again) tried to stab the new Pope with a bayonet and then **another** assassination attempt happened when John Paul 2 visited the Philippines.

Luckily Pope John Paul 2 would avoid any more would be assassin's and eventually died of natural causes in 2005.

His successor was much more to the liking of the Vatican officials as Joseph Ratzinger (known as Pope Benedict XVI) was a former Neo Nazi and a fully paid up member of the Hitler Youth!

London Bombings 7/7

Sometimes described as Britain's 9/11 the London Bombings of 7 July 2005 killed 56 people and injured a great many more when four bombs were detonated on London's public transport system.

Three bombs exploded in under a minute on three London Underground trains and another exploded on a Double Decker bus in nearby Tavistock Square. The bombs were detonated during early morning rush hour in a wicked attempt to kill as many innocent bystanders as possible.

The official story States that 4 Muslim suicide bombers carried out their attacks as revenge for Britain invading Iraq, 3 of the bombers were British born with parents from Pakistan and the other was a Muslim convert from Jamaica.

However soon after the bombings a great many people began to question the official account and in my opinion with very good reason.

To begin with how about the immaculate documentation belonging to the alleged bomber's that was found at the scene. How on earth did these pieces of paper survive such a strong blast?

Almost as if they were planted at the scene later (similar to how the terrorists of 9/11 were identified by their passports which somehow survived the plane crash into the World Trade Centre buildings even though both buildings and planes were vaporized).

Also the Security Services claimed that all 4 bombers were on a suicide mission. This is really very odd because on their journey traveling from West Yorkshire to London they purchased return train tickets.

Now if you were planning to carry out a suicide bombing why would you need to buy a return ticket?

Furthermore one of the alleged bombers Hasib Hussain attempted to phone the other 3 bombers after they had detonated their bombs. If they really were suicide bombers then surely he would have known that the other 3 bombers were already dead and would have no need to contact them (Hussain would get on a bus and detonate his bomb a short while later in Tavistock Square according to the official log).

Another anomaly relates to the train which authorities claimed was used by the bombers to get from West Yorkshire to London on the morning of the attacks. This train was actually cancelled!

Also very strange was some of the witness accounts especially from the people who were unfortunate enough to be on the train network during the attacks.

Indeed according to witness testimony and also based upon the photographic evidence of the blast damage it would appear much more likely that the bombs were placed on the tracks themselves. If this is really the case then surely the 4 Muslim men could not possibly be guilty but simply fall guys set up by the British government to take the blame.

Oddly Israeli Finance Minster Benjamin Netanyahu (now Prime Minister of Israel) was due to travel through the area of London that was affected by the bombings. However he must have had a premonition as the trip was cancelled 1 hour before the first 3 bombs exploded!

So if we accept that as per usual the official version of events are not all at accurate or in line with the evidence then what really happened? And why?

One very popular theory both at the time and at present relates to the mounting unpopularity of the illegal invasion of Iraq 2 years before.

By late 2004 and early 2005 the British population had really started to sour on the idea of the ongoing war in Iraq. It really was a rather senseless bloodbath and did nobody any good whatsoever (except for a few shady corporations who always come out of these things even richer).

The theory goes that the British government staged a fake terrorist attack in London in order to somehow justify the illegal Iraq invasion in 2003 (a sort of false flag if you will).

Another theory was that Mossad (Israeli Secret Service) had carried out the attack and framed the 4 muslim men in order to gain more popular support for their eternal struggle against various Muslim led countries.

Whatever the truth I am hopeful that some day we will know the truth, perhaps a death bed confession maybe?

UFO's

UFO's also known as Unidentified Flying Objects are essentially anything that is airborne which cannot be explained (meaning that is not a plane nor a species of bird).

Sightings of UFO's actually date back thousands of years with reports from ancient Egyptians and Romans depicted in various scrolls.

The modern era of UFO sightings really began in the 1940s during World War 2, a great many Allied pilots described seeing very odd and futuristic looking crafts over the war torn skies of Europe. These craft were usually known as 'Foo Fighter's.

The Allied pilots believed that these crafts were from Nazi Germany but after World War 2 had ended a number of German Air Force pilots (Luftwaffe) stated that they had also seen the odd looking craft and they believed them to be Allied crafts.

Soon after in 1947 a UFO was thought to have crash landed in the small town of Roswell in New Mexico. The Roswell Army Air Filed public information officer Walter Haut issued a press release stating that the Military had recovered "A Flying Disc".

The Army soon changed their story however saying that the crash debris was actually a weather balloon although a great many people were rightly skeptical of this explanation.

Several years later Jesse Marcel who was a highly decorated Flight Lieutenant Colonel in the United States Air Force gave an interview to a well respected UFO researcher named Stanton Friedman.

In the interview Jesse Marcel claimed that the debris found at Roswell during 1947 was Extraterrestrial in nature and that the Military had ordered a cover up. Some people also claimed that the Military had discovered several alien beings scattered around the debris and even had one of the aliens dissected. Indeed there was a black and white movie showing an apparent autopsy but later emerged that it was a fake.

I personally think that there was some sort of cover up at Roswell based on Jesse Marcel's interview alone. What would he have to gain by lying about this? He is a very strong witness and with his superb Military record he cannot simply be dismissed as a crank like so many other witnesses to UFO's sadly are.

Although most UFO sightings do seem to be based in North America there were many recorded sightings in other parts of the world including Great Britain. Interestingly my mum and aunty both witnessed a UFO way back in the early 1960s in Dover, Kent. According to my auntie several buses in the town centre actually stopped and pulled over in order for the passenger's
to get a closer look!

Probably the most famous ever case in Great Britain occurred on Boxing Day in 1980 in Rendlesham Forest in Suffolk. There was an American Air Force Base in the area which picked up an unidentified craft on their radar system.

As a result the base was put on Red Alert (this was still the Cold War era) and a patrol was sent out into the forest in order to investigate further. Several of the men on the patrol claimed to have witnessed incredible beams of blue and red lights which were emanating from a metallic craft that had actually landed in Rendlesham Forest.

The Commander of Base Gordon Williams stated that he approached the metallic craft and was actually able to communicate with some of the creatures onboard via sign language.

Some of the other men on patrol claimed to have seen some of the creatures carrying out repairs on the craft before it was able to take off again in a massive burst of both speed and light. Some of the local farmers later stated that some of their livestock were visibly distressed by this turn of events and many sadly ran out into the roads and were killed by passing traffic!

Naturally the American Airfare attempted to play down the incident insisting that it was of no importance but even they could not really explain why it was that so many trees were either totally destroyed or damaged during the night or why the radiation levels on the site were so incredibly high.

Every year there are thousands of sightings all around the world from a wide variety of people from all different walks of life and their testimonies cannot be easily ignored.

Also a great many famous people have also witnessed such strange crafts including Actor Dan Ackroyd, Rock and Roll legend Elvis Presley and respected American Broadcaster Walter Cronkite.

Whether these crafts are from outer space or maybe from somewhere closer to home it is clear to most people that currently Science just cannot provide a satisfactory explanation for their present.

The Death of Princess Diana

On 31 August 1997 The Princess of Wales Lady Diana Spencer died in an apparent car accident in the French capital city of Paris.

The official story is that Henri Paul (who was driving the Mercedes that Diana and her boyfriend Dodi Fayed were travelling in) lost control of the vehicle whilst trying to escape some rather overzealous Paparazzi photographers.

The apparent accident occurred during the early hours of Sunday 31 August 1997 in the Post De L'alma Tunnel in Paris.

Trevor Rees Jones who was the bodyguard of Princess Diana was also in the car at the time and although badly injured he did survive happily.

The controlled British media generally blamed everything on Princess Diana and Dodi Fayed's driver claiming that he was a drunk driver.

For me this is clearly inaccurate as Henri Paul (who also worked as the Deputy Security Chief at the Ritz Hotel) was seen on CCTV footage at the Ritz shortly before the crash and he showed no signs at all of being drunk.

I find it very unlikely that a high class establishment such as the Ritz would employ somebody who was a drunkard as a Deputy Security Chief. Also if he really was drunk as the media claimed then surely Princess Diana or Dodi would have not allowed him to drive them in the first place.

Minutes after the crash had occurred a French Doctor arrived at the scene and immediately began treating Princess Diana (Dodi sadly died instantly and could not be saved). In an interview given soon afterwards the Doctor said that although Princess Diana's injuries were indeed serious he was really shocked that she had died as a result of them.

It later emerged that the ambulance that attended the scene did not take Princess

Diana to the nearby Hospital (Hotel Dieu) but instead took her to Pitie Salpetriere Hospital which was some miles away.

This critical delay could easily have been the difference between life and death for the popular Princess.

The official story says that Princess Diana's vehicle most probably collided with a white Fiat Uno that was spotted by several witnesses at the time. A Vietnamese born man by the name of Le Van Thanh was almost certainly the driver of the vehicle.

Le Van Thanh gave his account of the incident several years ago to an author who was researching the case for a book.

Le Van Thanh stated that the French police knew he was involved but swore him to secrecy and warned him not to speak to the investigating British Authorities (although they need not have worried as the British Authorities would most likely have blamed it on Putin).

So if we accept that as per usual the official story is clearly false than what did really happen?

Was the Princess assassinated? And if so for what reason? Was poor Dodi simply just collateral damage?

Well Princess Diana had Made some very powerful enemies since divorcing Prince Charles (now sadly King) not least the British Security Services. Now free of the Royal shackles Diana could freely give her opinion on subjects which previously would have been taboo (including Charles various affairs), for these reasons Diana was maybe seen as something of a loose cannon that had to be dealt with.

Another powerful enemy of Princess Diana was the various shady corporations that directly benefit from the sale of weapons. This was due to Diana in early 1997 beginning a very successful campaign against the use of landmines.

The gutsy Princess even walked a cross an active landmine field in Angola with a number of de-miners clearing away explosives. This directly led to a treaty soon afterwards called 'The Ottawa Mines Treaty'. This treaty actively discouraged the sale and use of landmines.

This was great news for 99% of the population but bad news for scum of the earth arms dealers, maybe they wanted revenge for their loss of revenue!

In 2004 a new inquiry was launched looking into the sad death of Princess Diana and Dodi Fayed, although sadly it was chaired by dead beat former Police Commissioner John Stevens.

John Stevens after 2 years of 'work' came to the conclusion that the original story was 100% correct in a move which should have surprised nobody.

Dodi Fayed's father Mohammed Al-Fayed (owner of Harrods and at the time Fulham Football Club) was rightly very skeptical of the inquiry. Mr Al-Fayed believe very strongly that his son and Princess Diana were murdered in cold blood by forces working on behalf of the British Crown.

Mr Al-Fayed also suggested that Princess Diana was pregnant with Dodo's baby at the time of the crash.

Naturally the vile reptiles that make up most of the British media attacked Mr Al-Fayed as some sort of Conspiracy Theorist but I would say that he was simply questioning the account of proven liars and attempting to obtain some sort of justice for both the death of his son Dodi and the late great Princess Diana.

Most of the media attacked Mr Al-Fayed making him out to be some sort of criminal, naturally they failed to mention his charity that helps children living with disabilities or the school he helped fund for children with special needs.

Sadly I fear that at this point we may Never know the truth of what really happened that fateful night in France only that the official story as usual bears no resemblance to the evidence.

Well there we have it a look at some of my favorite Conspiracy Theories from years gone by. I hope you enjoyed this book and maybe even found it thought provoking (thoughts such as why did I buy this book?).

If by chance you did enjoy this book and if you are a fan of video games then please check out some of my other books which are on sale via Amazon.co.uk including Console Gaming in The 1990s and Arcade Gaming in The 1990s.

Thanks once again to everyone who managed to read this book (all 3 of you), see you all soon
hopefully.

Eric Bowden